Trains

Stephanie Turnbull

Designed by Neil Francis,
Catherine-Anne MacKinnon & Jayne Wilson

Illustrated by John Woodcock
Consultants: David Williams & John J. Morena

Contents

Internet links

For links to the websites recommended in this book, go to the **Usborne Quicklinks Website** at **www.usborne-quicklinks.com** and enter the keywords "discovery trains". Usborne Publishing is not responsible for the content on any website other than its own. Please read the internet safety guidelines on the Usborne Quicklinks Website and on page 46 of this book.

★ Pictures in this book with a star symbol beside them can be downloaded for your own personal use from the Usborne Quicklinks Website

Title page: Japanese high-speed bullet trains
Left: A crowded steam train travels along the narrow, winding Darjeeling Railway in India.

Train basics

The invention of trains, about two hundred years ago, transformed the world. Before trains, journeys were slow and difficult. People had to use horses to get around and to carry goods. Steam trains and, later, diesel and electric trains have linked towns and cities around the world and provided us with a fast, and often exciting, way to travel.

Train parts

A train is made up of wagons or carriages (also called cars) pulled by a locomotive, which is an engine on wheels. Steam locomotives also pull a wagon called a tender, containing fuel.

Steam power

The first steam locomotives were designed in the early 1800s. They were built to transport all kinds of goods quickly and easily, but train companies soon realized that trains could carry passengers too. Steam trains ran on railways all over the world for more than a hundred years.

This British steam train has been kept in good working order.

Sturdy diesels

Diesel trains began to replace steam trains around sixty years ago. Their engines work in the same way as truck engines, but they use oil rather than petrol (gasoline). Diesel engines are very powerful, and they often haul long trains over enormous distances.

Modern diesel trains, like this one, often have high, rounded fronts. The driver sits very high up and has a good view of the track ahead.

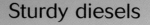

Internet links

For links to websites where you can find train games, video clips, puzzles and things to make and do, and learn more about the history of trains, go to **www.usborne-quicklinks.com**

Speedy electrics

The fastest modern trains are powered by electricity, which is transmitted to the trains from overhead lines. Many electric trains that run underground work slightly differently. Their electric power comes from an extra rail alongside the track.

This is a type of electric train known as a bullet train. Its slim, smooth shape and pointed nose help it zoom along at speeds of around 270kph (170mph).

Fact: The world record for the fastest train is held by an electric train called a TGV Atlantique. In 1990 it reached a speed of 515kph (320mph).

The first trains

The earliest steam locomotives were heavy, slow machines. They could pull heavy loads, but they moved no faster than a horse, and they often broke down.

This picture from 1809 shows the locomotive *Catch Me Who Can* being displayed on a circular track.

Early designs

The first steam locomotive was built in 1804 by an English engineer named Richard Trevithick. But it wasn't a successful design, as the locomotive was so heavy it broke the track. Trevithick's next locomotive was called *Catch Me Who Can*. This worked better, as it was much lighter.

Locomotion

In 1825, an engineer named George Stephenson built a railway in northern England. At the railway's opening ceremony, he displayed a locomotive he had designed, called *Locomotion*. This locomotive was used on the railway to haul coal wagons.

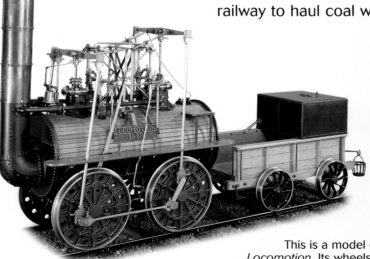

This is a model of *Locomotion*. Its wheels had raised edges, which helped it to stay firmly on the rails.

A winning design

In 1829, George Stephenson invented an even better locomotive. It was called *Rocket* and it was designed to take part in a competition. A new railway had been built, and a contest was held to choose a locomotive to run on it. *Rocket* won easily. Not only was it the fastest locomotive, but it was the only one that didn't break down.

How *Rocket* worked

The diagrams below show how *Rocket* worked. The first shows how steam was made, and the second shows how this turned the wheels.

A coal fire burned in the firebox, which heated water in a boiler. As the water boiled it produced steam, which flowed into a cylinder.

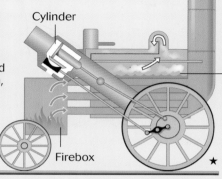

Cylinder

Boiler

Firebox

Steam filled the cylinder and pushed down a metal disc called a piston. The piston was connected to a rod that turned the wheels.

The steam then went out through the exhaust pipe, and the piston moved back up.

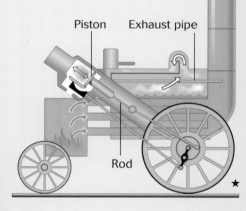

Piston   Exhaust pipe

Rod

This locomotive is a replica of *Rocket* as it looked in 1829.

Internet link

For a link to a website where you can rebuild *The Rocket* online and play a quiz game about early trains, go to **www.usborne-quicklinks.com**

Fact: *Rocket* was such a reliable, well-built locomotive that all steam locomotives since have had the same basic design.

Steaming ahead

Railways became very popular from about 1830. Soon they were being built all over the world, and new, improved steam locomotives were running on them.

Steam goes global

At first, foreign companies bought British locomotives, but they soon began to build their own. France, Switzerland and Germany were the first countries outside Britain to design their own locomotives.

Internet link

For a link to a website where you can follow the development of the railway in Britain and explore an animated map, go to **www.usborne-quicklinks.com**

This locomotive is an exact copy of *Der Adler*, the first steam locomotive to run in Germany.

Track types

The distance between the two rails of a track is called the gauge. Many of the first railways had a standard gauge of 1.4m (4ft, 8.5in).

A narrow gauge   Standard gauge   A wide gauge

Some later railways had wider gauges, which helped keep trains more stable. Narrow railways were also built. These were often used in rough terrain where railway-building was difficult. Today, most railways use the standard gauge, but wider and narrower gauges still exist.

Fact: Railway owners made a lot of money. One English businessman, named George Hudson, became so rich that he was known as the "Railway King".

This is *Fairy Queen*, the oldest working steam locomotive in the world. It was built in Britain in 1855 and taken to India, where it still runs.

Big and small wheels

There are three types of steam locomotive wheels. The most important wheels are driving wheels. These are the large, main wheels that are turned by pistons and that move the locomotive. All steam locomotives have driving wheels.

Some locomotives also have small front wheels known as leading wheels. These help to guide the locomotive forward. Locomotives can also have small back wheels called trailing wheels. These help to carry the weight of the firebox and the driver's cab.

Wheel codes

The number and type of wheels a steam locomotive has is usually written as a "wheel code". Here are a few examples.

This locomotive is a 4-4-2. It has four leading wheels, four driving wheels and two trailing wheels.

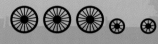

A 4-6-0 has four leading wheels, six driving wheels and no trailing wheels.

This locomotive is known as a 2-8-2. Can you see why?

American railroads

The first American railways, or railroads as they are called in the U.S.A., were built in the 1830s. Railroads changed the country forever. They enabled people to travel farther than ever before, often across vast areas of rocky, rough terrain.

Internet links

For links to websites where you can watch movies about steam engines and the growth of railroads in the U.S.A., go to **www.usborne-quicklinks.com**

Lightweight locos

The U.S.A. is a huge country, and railroad builders soon found that it was very expensive to build such long railroads. So, to keep costs low, they made tracks from cheap, lightweight materials. They then designed light locomotives that could run on the tracks without breaking them.

Out of the way!

Many early American railroads ran through open land where cows and other animals grazed. Sometimes animals wandered onto the track. Locomotives had a whistle and a bell that the driver could sound to scare animals away. If this didn't work, animals were knocked out of the way by a row of bars, called a cowcatcher, or pilot, on the front of the locomotive.

An American train steams through the Colorado countryside. The locomotive was built to transport gold and silver from nearby mines. Today, it takes tourists on scenic trips.

The American

The picture above shows the arrangement of wheels on a typical American steam locomotive.

The most common American steam locomotives were 4-4-0s. This meant that they had four small leading wheels and four large driving wheels. More than 25,000 were built, and this style of locomotive became known as "the American".

Union Pacific Railroad

The Union Pacific Railroad opened in 1869 and runs all the way across the U.S.A. It was the first railroad to cross a whole continent. One railroad company built the eastern half and another built the western half. There was no set meeting point and, as each company wanted to build the biggest section, they just kept building. The lines ran side by side for miles before an official meeting place was decided on.

This steam locomotive ran on the Union Pacific Railroad in 1869. Its huge cowcatcher pushed away any obstructions on the line ahead.

Fact: In 1830, an American steam locomotive called *Tom Thumb* raced against a horse to see which was faster. *Tom Thumb* broke down and the horse won.

Making tracks

Building a railway is a long, difficult process. Tracks must be laid on flat ground because it is hard for trains to climb slopes. This means that builders have to clear rocks and other obstacles to create a level route. Bridges are constructed over rivers and valleys.

Laying the track

The pictures below show how early railway tracks were laid. Although modern tracks look similar to these, they are built using stronger, longer-lasting materials.

A bed of crushed stones, called ballast, was laid. This created a firm base. Long pieces of wood, called sleepers or ties, were laid over the ballast.

Ballast

Sleeper or tie

Iron or steel rails were laid on top and held in place by iron supports called chairs. These were fixed to the sleepers, or ties.

Rail

Chair

★

Internet links

For links to websites where you can trace the building of railways across the US and Australia, and see Forth Bridge photos, go to **www.usborne-quicklinks.com**

Building bridges

Building a railway bridge is a long, difficult job, involving hundreds of workers. The bridge has to be strong enough to take the weight of long, heavy freight trains and solid enough to withstand the vibrations trains make as they thunder along. The first railway bridges were made of stone, but later, sturdier materials such as iron and steel were used.

This is the Forth Railway Bridge in Scotland, which opened in 1890. It was the first bridge to be made mainly of steel and is one of the strongest bridges ever built.

A dangerous job

Early railway builders faced all kinds of dangers. Some became sick from breathing in rock dust and poisonous fumes from explosives, and many were killed by mistimed dynamite blasts or by falling rocks.

Workers on the Union Pacific Railroad were sometimes attacked by Native Americans who were angry at seeing a railroad built across their land. In Africa, a few unlucky men were killed by lions.

This photograph, taken in the 1860s, shows workers laying tracks for the Union Pacific Railroad.

Fact: Workers began to build the Hoosac Tunnel in the U.S.A. in 1854. The rock was so hard to drill through that the tunnel took 24 years to finish.

All aboard

Journeying by steam train was a great adventure, taking people to places they had never been to before. But train trips could often be uncomfortable, unless passengers paid for expensive tickets.

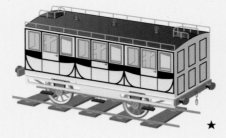

Early first class carriages, or cars, were solidly built and ornately decorated. There were many windows to look through.

Different classes

The first passenger trains had three types of carriages, or cars: first class, second class and third class. First class was the most expensive, with soft seats and plenty of room for luggage. Second class was cheaper and less spacious, while third class was very cheap and crowded, and sometimes had no seats at all.

Second class carriages, or cars, had a simpler design, with less decoration and fewer windows.

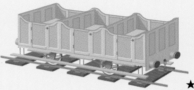

Third class carriages, or cars, were very basic. Until the 1840s, some didn't even have roofs.

The Orient Express

Only the wealthiest passengers could afford to travel on the Orient Express, a luxury train service that ran between France and Turkey, stopping at many cities on the way. It had restaurants, bars and sleeping cars, as well as plush salon cars with leather armchairs, velvet curtains and thick rugs.

The Orient Express service ran from 1883 until 1977. The trains are now owned by a new company, which offers trips to some cities on the original route.

Waiters on board the modern Orient Express

Fact: Early steam train drivers had to stand for the entire journey, in open cabs that left them exposed to the weather as well as smoke from the locomotive.

Palaces on wheels

The most luxurious passenger cars were those built for kings and queens. In the 1890s, Queen Victoria rode in grand coaches with padded silk walls and elegant furniture, as shown here. Emperor Napoleon III of France rode in style too. He had a private train with a balcony and wine storage area.

In the city ....

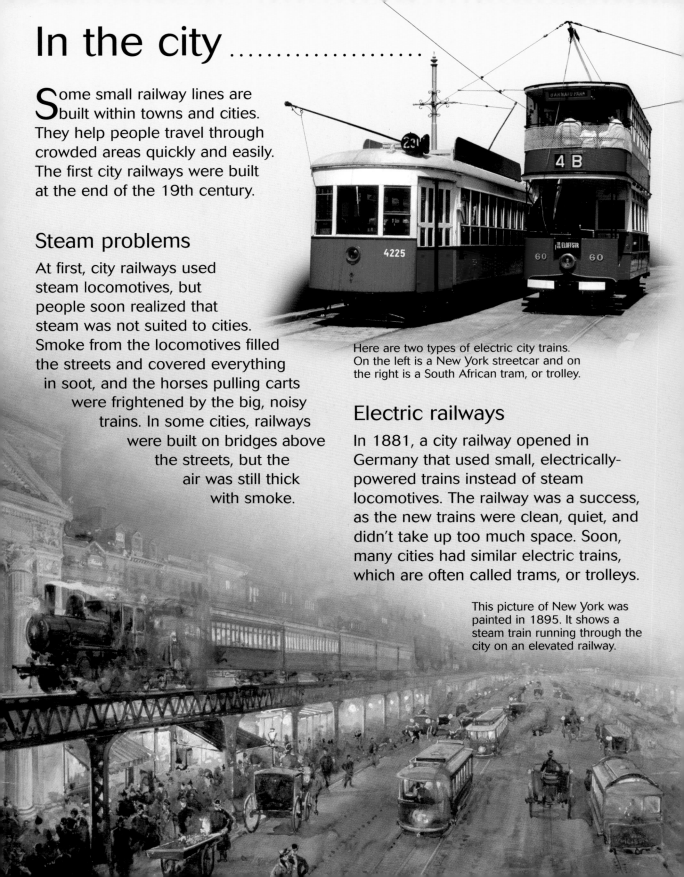

Some small railway lines are built within towns and cities. They help people travel through crowded areas quickly and easily. The first city railways were built at the end of the 19th century.

Steam problems

At first, city railways used steam locomotives, but people soon realized that steam was not suited to cities. Smoke from the locomotives filled the streets and covered everything in soot, and the horses pulling carts were frightened by the big, noisy trains. In some cities, railways were built on bridges above the streets, but the air was still thick with smoke.

Here are two types of electric city trains. On the left is a New York streetcar and on the right is a South African tram, or trolley.

Electric railways

In 1881, a city railway opened in Germany that used small, electrically-powered trains instead of steam locomotives. The railway was a success, as the new trains were clean, quiet, and didn't take up too much space. Soon, many cities had similar electric trains, which are often called trams, or trolleys.

This picture of New York was painted in 1895. It shows a steam train running through the city on an elevated railway.

Power from above

Electric trains usually get their electricity supply from overhead power lines. The trains have metal arms on the roof that touch the line and pick up electricity. This power is used to run a motor inside the train.

This picture shows how the arm on an electric train touches a power line.

Internet links

For links to websites where you can see photos of trams in different countries and watch a movie about monorails around the world, go to **www.usborne-quicklinks.com**

Trains on one rail

Another type of electric city train is the monorail, which runs on just one rail. Monorails are powered by electricity running through the rail. Their tracks are built high above the streets, out of the way of all the traffic below.

Some monorails hang below the rail rather than riding on top of it. These are called suspended monorails.

This is the Shonan suspended monorail in Japan. It glides high above the busy streets.

Fact: One of the oldest and most famous monorails is in Wuppertal, Germany. The 13km (8-mile) line was built in 1901 and is still used today.

17

Going underground

T he first underground railway opened
in London in 1863. London's streets
were very crowded, and the railway was
a faster way of getting around. By 1900
there were similar underground railways
in Budapest, Boston and Paris.

The Metropolitan

This shows what the Metropolitan Railway steam
locomotives looked like. They were all painted red.

The first London Underground line was
called the Metropolitan Railway. It was
6km (4 miles) long. At first, Metropolitan
trains were pulled by steam
locomotives. But these were too
smoky to be used in narrow
tunnels, and they were
soon replaced by
electric trains.

Building tunnels

The first London Underground tunnels
were built just below the ground.
Workers dug a trench in the road and
laid railway lines in it. These were then
covered with an arched, brick roof,
and the road was rebuilt over the top.
This way of building tunnels was known
as the "cut and cover" method.

Later railway tunnels were built much
deeper underground, using special
tunnel-boring equipment. This was
a much better method as it meant
that workers didn't have to dig up
roads. The London Underground
was nicknamed the "Tube" because
of these round, tube-like tunnels.

A modern electric train running
through one of the deep, tube-
like tunnels in the London
Underground system

Fact: The largest underground network in the world is the New York City Subway.
It has 1,355km (842 miles) of track, some of which runs above the ground.

Huge chandeliers light up this Moscow Metro station.

Underground palaces

The Moscow Metro was built in the 1930s and is famous for its beautiful stations. The greatest Russian architects designed the stations, which have high, arched ceilings with elaborate decoration.

The stations look stunning, but the people who built them had a terrible time. They had to work long, gruelling hours, often in freezing weather. Many workers died because of these hardships.

Internet links

For links to websites where you can see photos of the Metropolitan Railway's steam engine and find out about the world's largest underground systems, go to **www.usborne-quicklinks.com**

The Métro

One of the most famous underground networks is the Paris Métro. It opened in 1900 with just one railway line. Today it has 15 lines and more than 300 stations.

A few Métro stations have beautiful entrances. These were designed by an architect named Hector Guimard. He used glass and iron to create graceful, curved railings and signs. This style of art is known as Art Nouveau.

This Paris Métro entrance has an elaborate glass canopy above it.

Mountain trains

Some trains travel high into the mountains. The tracks are often long and winding, as many trains can't climb very steep slopes.

Into the clouds

The Andes mountain range in South America has some of the highest railways in the world. One line, named the Peruvian Central, climbs to over 4,800m (15,750ft). The rise is so steep that trains carry emergency bottles of oxygen in case passengers have difficulty breathing.

A train emerges from a mountain in the Andes. Tunnels are built through mountains that are too steep for trains to climb.

Climbing the Himalayas

This picture shows a loop of track on the Darjeeling Railway. It allows the train to climb hills easily.

The Darjeeling Railway in India weaves through the Himalaya mountains. It climbs about 2,000m (6,560ft). The track loops and zigzags up the mountains, so that the steam train doesn't have to tackle steep slopes. The railway opened in 1881, and steam trains still run on it today.

Rack-and-pinion

Rack-and-pinion railways run up steep hills. They have an extra rail (the rack) in the middle of the track, with grooves cut into it. Locomotives that use the railway have an extra, grooved wheel (the pinion) that slots into the rail. This helps the locomotives grip the track and pull themselves up the hill.

This rack railway runs to Gornergrat, the highest railway station in Switzerland.

This shows how the grooved wheel of a rack-and-pinion railway slots into the gaps in the rail.

Funicular railways

For even steeper slopes, funicular railways are used. These railways have cables that pull passenger cars up the steep track. There are usually two tracks, with a car on each. While one car is pulled up, the other is lowered. The cables are operated by a steam engine or an electric motor.

Funicular trains can climb extremely steep slopes. This electric funicular takes passengers up the Niesen mountain in Switzerland.

Faster and faster

By the 1930s, many cars were being built. Railway companies worried that soon no one would travel by train. They began to design more powerful steam locomotives to haul faster trains, which they hoped would attract more passengers.

Internet link

For a link to a website where you can explore an online guide to *The Flying Scotsman* and watch a video clip, go to **www.usborne-quicklinks.com**

The Flying Scotsman is still in good working order, and it often runs at special train events.

Flying along

One of the fastest 1930s locomotives was *The Flying Scotsman*. It was built in Britain and pulled the first non-stop train from London to Edinburgh, a distance of 632km (393 miles). At the time, this was the longest non-stop run ever made.

In 1934, *The Flying Scotsman* broke another record. This time it became the first locomotive to reach a recorded speed of 160kph (100mph). This started a worldwide race to set new locomotive speed records.

Fact: In 1989, *The Flying Scotsman* again broke the world record for the longest non-stop run by a steam locomotive, covering 679km (422 miles).

Record breakers

Many steam locomotives soon broke *The Flying Scotsman*'s speed record. By 1936, the world's fastest steam locomotive was the German No. 05001, which reached 199kph (124mph).

Then, in 1938, a new British steam locomotive named *Mallard* set a world record of 202kph (126mph). This speed has never been beaten by a steam locomotive.

This is the sleek, blue *Mallard*, which ran on British railways for 25 years.

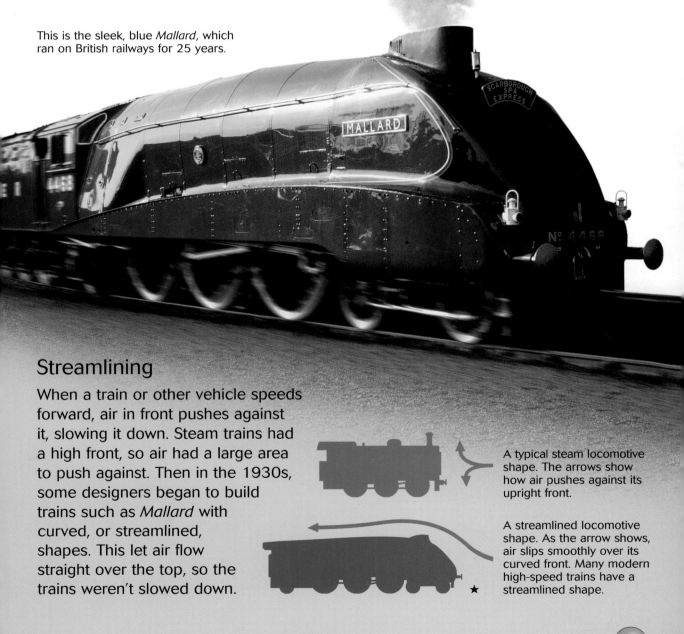

Streamlining

When a train or other vehicle speeds forward, air in front pushes against it, slowing it down. Steam trains had a high front, so air had a large area to push against. Then in the 1930s, some designers began to build trains such as *Mallard* with curved, or streamlined, shapes. This let air flow straight over the top, so the trains weren't slowed down.

A typical steam locomotive shape. The arrows show how air pushes against its upright front.

A streamlined locomotive shape. As the arrow shows, air slips smoothly over its curved front. Many modern high-speed trains have a streamlined shape.

Diesel power

From the 1930s onwards, diesel locomotives began to replace steam locomotives. They were cheaper to run and used less fuel. Diesels could also run at higher speeds.

This Santa Fe diesel has a distinctive red and yellow logo on its front.

Diesel and electric

Although diesel locomotives use oil as fuel, it is electricity that drives the wheels. The diesel engine powers a device called a generator, which creates electricity. The electricity runs small motors, which turn the wheels.

This is a cutaway diagram of a typical diesel locomotive. It has a diesel engine, a generator to produce electricity, and a motor to turn each wheel.

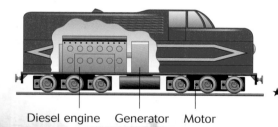

Diesel engine   Generator   Motor

American style

Many diesels are stylishly designed. The American Zephyr diesels of the 1930s had shiny, silver bodies made of steel. In the 1950s, diesels on the Santa Fe Railroad in the U.S.A. were famous for their bright red and yellow logo.

Fact: The world record for the fastest diesel-powered train is held by a British Intercity 125. In 1987, it reached a speed of 238kph (148mph).

Deltic diesels

Diesel power was first used in Britain in the 1960s. The most famous early British diesels were called Deltics. They were able to reach a top speed of 169kph (105mph). This was faster than any other train in Britain at that time.

On the right is the first Deltic ever built. There were 22 Deltics in total, and they operated on routes between London and the north of England.

Internet links

For links to websites where you can take a virtual tour of an American diesel locomotive and find out what it's like to drive one, go to **www.usborne-quicklinks.com**

Trans-Europe Express

In 1957, a high-speed diesel service began in Europe. It was called the Trans-Europe Express, and it linked France, Germany, Italy, Switzerland and the Netherlands. Trans-Europe Express trains were bright red with long, rounded fronts. They were designed for luxury travel, and were expensive to travel on.

A Trans-Europe Express diesel train speeds through Germany.

Cargo carriers

Trains are a fast, efficient way of moving goods. Over the years, trains have carried all kinds of cargo, from coal to chemicals. Goods are carried in open trucks or sealed containers which are loaded onto flat trailers.

A steam-powered freight train transports coal and other goods across South Africa.

Food transporters

Today, specially refrigerated trucks are used to carry fresh goods such as fruit, vegetables, meat and fish. But before refrigerators were invented, fresh food was carried in ice-filled trucks. When the ice began to melt, the train had to stop at an "icing station" to stock up on ice.

★

Ice hatch

Steps to hatch

Early fresh food trucks looked like this. Ice was loaded into the truck though a hatch in the roof.

Longer and longer

Today, freight trains are usually hauled by diesel locomotives. Often, several locomotives are linked together so that many extra wagons can be added. The longest freight train ever had 660 wagons. It was pulled by 16 diesel locomotives for a single journey of 7km (4 miles) in South Africa in 1989.

Mail trains

Before planes and fast road vehicles were used to transport mail, people relied on trains. Mail trains often picked up mail without stopping. Mail bags were hung from hooks by the track. As the train came past, the bags were caught in a net on the side of the train.

Workers on board the train then sorted the mail. They bagged up the letters and hung them outside the train. The bags were caught in a net on the platform edge.

Mail bags hang from a hook, ready to fall into the train's net.

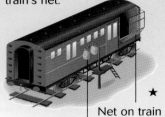

★

Net on train

Mail bag

A net on the platform is ready to catch a bag of sorted mail.

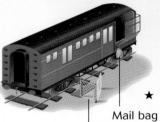

★

Mail bag

Net on platform

Underground mail

London has an underground postal service, which has been running since 1927. Driverless electric trains pull loaded mail wagons to large post offices where the mail is sorted. The trains are now operated by computers.

One of London's underground mail trains

A diesel-powered freight train travels through Wyoming, U.S.A. The long train curves around to the left.

Internet links

For links to websites where you can see photos of cargo trains and read about London's underground postal service, go to www.usborne-quicklinks.com

Fact: The heaviest freight train ever weighed more than 70,000 tonnes (69,000 tons). It was so heavy because it was transporting iron.

Steam giants

The biggest steam locomotives of all were built in the 1940s. These heavy, powerful engines could haul huge loads over long distances.

Internet links

For a link to a website where you can find photographs and facts about powerful steam locomotives, go to www.usborne-quicklinks.com

Kings of the track

The most famous steam giants were Union Pacific Big Boy locomotives. Big Boys were twice as long as most locomotives, and they each had the power to haul 100 loaded wagons. They could go as fast as 110kph (70mph) on flat stretches of track.

This Big Boy towers 5m (16ft) above the track. The locomotive is almost the height of three adults, standing on each others' shoulders.

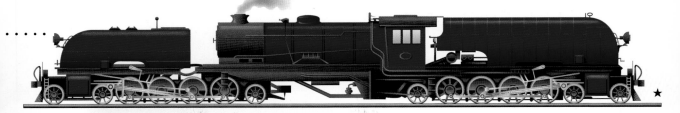

Double the power

The biggest steam locomotives, such as Big Boys, had two sets of driving wheels instead of one (see page 9). This gave them extra power to haul heavy loads and climb steep slopes. These extra-long locomotives could usually do the work of two or three smaller locomotives.

Built to last

Steam giants were so solid and strong that they lasted for many years. Some huge locomotives made by a British company called Beyer-Garratt are still used in parts of Africa to carry coal and other goods.

This picture shows a Beyer-Garratt locomotive. It has a total of 16 big driving wheels, making it one of the world's longest and most powerful locomotives.

War trains

Many large locomotives were built in the Second World War to transport vital supplies of fuel, food and weapons to soldiers. These locomotives needed to be sturdy enough to run along uneven, bomb-damaged tracks.

Heavy tanks being carried by train during the Second World War

High-speed electrics

Fast electric trains were first built in the 1950s, and could travel far faster than steam or diesel trains. Electric trains were designed for long-distance passenger journeys, to compete with airline companies which had begun to offer flights to many destinations.

Internet link

For a link to a website where you can watch a slide show about bullet trains, go to **www.usborne-quicklinks.com**

The first designs

The earliest high-speed electric trains were developed in Europe. These trains could reach speeds of 130kph (80mph). Many were stylish and luxurious, and some only had first class carriages, or cars, so tickets were very expensive.

But there was a problem with these high-speed trains, as they had to share railway lines with slower passenger and freight trains. This meant that they were rarely able to run at full speed.

This is an Italian train called the Settebello. In the 1950s it was Italy's fastest train.

This Japanese bullet train has a streamlined front that helps it cut through the air easily.

Fact: Passengers on the Italian Settebello train could sit right at the front of the train and look out at the track ahead. The driver sat in a small cab above.

Speeding bullets

In 1964, a railway line opened in Japan that was built specially for high-speed trains. It ran between Tokyo and Osaka. The electric trains used on the line were able to travel at a maximum speed of 210kph (130mph).

These Japanese trains were nicknamed bullet trains, not only because they were so fast, but because they were shaped like bullets. More Japanese high-speed lines have since been built, along with new, faster bullet trains.

A French success

Europe's first railway line reserved for high-speed trains opened in France in 1982. It linked Paris in the north with Lyons in the south, and used streamlined new trains called *Trains à Grande Vitesse*, or TGVs for short.

TGVs had an average speed of 270kph (168mph) and were so fast and convenient to use that they soon attracted thousands of passengers. More TGV lines were built, and soon similar high-speed lines were being created across the world.

High-speed tracks are as straight as possible, with no curves to slow down the trains.

This is one of the first TGVs. It still runs in south-east France.

The end of steam? ....

Today, most countries use diesel or electric trains, which are more efficient than steam trains. But steam still survives in a few countries, such as China and South Africa, while in some other parts of the world steam trains are restored and run on small, tourist railways.

The metal panels on the sides of this Chinese steam locomotive are smoke deflectors. They channel air up and force smoke away from the driver's cab.

Internet links

For links to websites where you can listen to steam train sounds and see pictures of restored steam trains, go to **www.usborne-quicklinks.com**

Chinese steam

Steam trains have been used in China for years, because the country has a lot of coal for fuel. But steam is now seen as old-fashioned, and no new steam locomotives have been built since 1982. Today, China has fewer than 3,000 steam locomotives, compared with 12,000 diesel and electric locomotives.

前进 ☉ 1364

Moving museums

There are many people who think that steam trains are far more beautiful and exciting than modern trains, and they want to make sure that these trains never disappear completely. Many groups of steam enthusiasts repair, repaint and run old steam locomotives for the enjoyment of steam fans of all ages.

A steam train on the Bluebell Railway in southern England. The line is owned by a group of steam enthusiasts, who run restored steam trains on it.

Fact: A few companies still produce small numbers of steam locomotives. For example, eight steam locomotives were recently built for Swiss tourist railways.

Under the sea

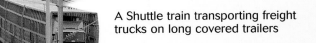

A few railway lines are built in tunnels that run deep under the sea. The longest underwater railway is the Channel tunnel, which lies under the English Channel and links Britain and France.

A Shuttle train transporting freight trucks on long covered trailers

The Channel tunnel

The Channel tunnel system has three tunnels, each about 50km (30 miles) long. There are two main rail tunnels, plus a service tunnel in the middle. This is linked to the other tunnels by passageways, and is used by engineers when they carry out track repairs.

The tunnels opened in 1994 after eight years of building work. Special boring equipment was used to create the tunnels, which lie 40m (130ft) below the seabed.

Shuttle trains

The trains that carry trucks, cars, coaches and motorcycles between Britain and France are called Shuttles. Passengers stay with their vehicles the whole time. At the end of the journey they drive off the train and straight onto a road.

This diagram shows the three tunnels under the Channel.

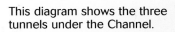

Tunnel for trains to Britain

Service tunnel

Tunnel for trains to France

This tunnel-boring machine was used to cut through the soil and rock under the English Channel.

Eurostar

Eurostar trains run a high-speed passenger service between London and Paris. The journey takes just three hours, which is less than half the time the same trip takes using ordinary trains and a ferry to cross the Channel.

Eurostar trains are designed in the same way as French TGVs (see page 31). The trains have 18 carriages, or cars, and can carry 770 passengers, almost as many as two jumbo jet aircraft.

A new undersea tunnel

Another rail link that joins two countries is the Øresund tunnel and bridge. The link opened in 2000 and connects Denmark and Sweden. Trains leaving Denmark run through a tunnel below the sea for 4km (2.5 miles), then come up onto a specially-built island. The trains then cross the rest of the way to Sweden on a bridge.

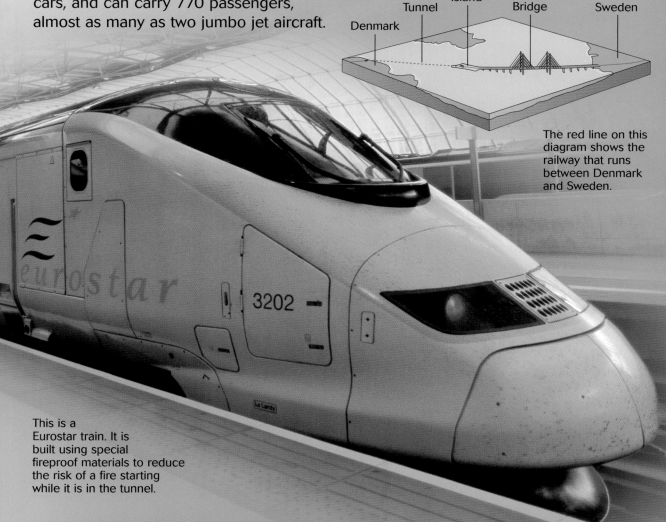

Denmark | Tunnel | Island | Bridge | Sweden

The red line on this diagram shows the railway that runs between Denmark and Sweden.

This is a Eurostar train. It is built using special fireproof materials to reduce the risk of a fire starting while it is in the tunnel.

3202

Fact: Every day, about 360 train journeys are made under the sea between Britain and France.

Modern machines . . . .

Train designers and engineers are constantly working to develop new, improved trains that are faster, sleeker and more efficient than ever.

Tilting trains

Trains that run on tracks with bends and curves can't travel as fast as trains on straight tracks, because they have to slow down to go around bends. If they didn't slow down, passengers would be flung to one side as the train turned.

Now trains have been designed that tilt slightly as they go around a bend. This means that they can keep up a high speed without passengers even noticing that the train is turning.

The Thalys above runs to stations between Paris, Brussels and Amsterdam. Thalys trains are often nicknamed "red trains" as they have red seats as well as a red exterior.

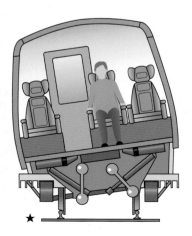

This cutaway diagram shows a train tilting as it turns a bend. The wheels stay firmly on the track. Passengers don't notice the tilt, or the bend in the track.

New TGVs

Many of the fastest modern trains are TGVs. One of the best new TGV types is called the Thalys. Thalys trains have a top speed of 300kph (186mph). They are jointly owned by train companies in France, Belgium, Holland and Germany, and they regularly run on routes through all four countries.

Fact: In 2001, a French TGV set a record for the fastest 1,000km (620-mile) trip. It ran from Calais to Marseilles at an average speed of 306kph (190mph).

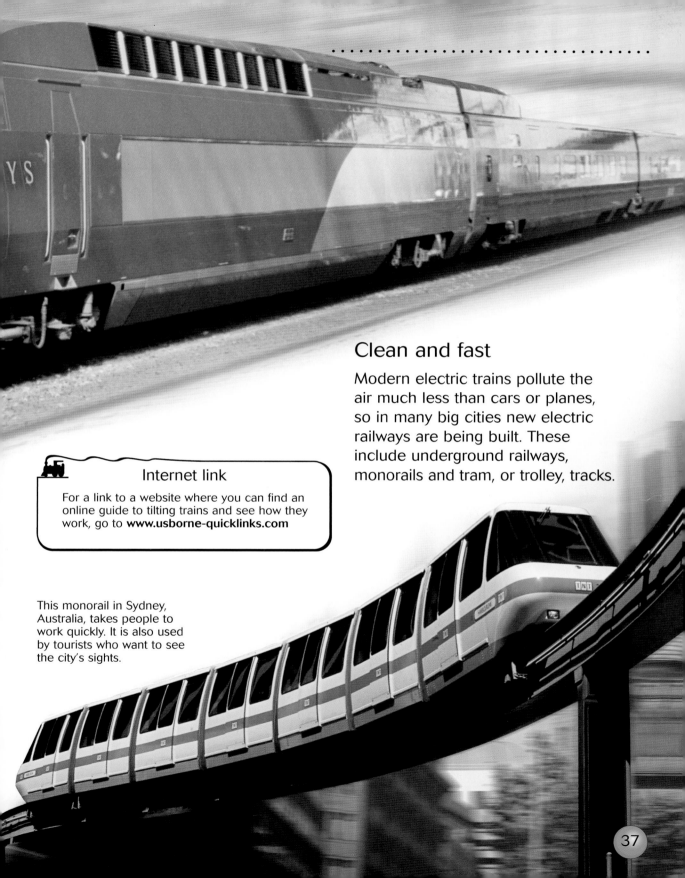

Clean and fast

Modern electric trains pollute the air much less than cars or planes, so in many big cities new electric railways are being built. These include underground railways, monorails and tram, or trolley, tracks.

Internet link

For a link to a website where you can find an online guide to tilting trains and see how they work, go to **www.usborne-quicklinks.com**

This monorail in Sydney, Australia, takes people to work quickly. It is also used by tourists who want to see the city's sights.

Floating trains

New trains are now being built that don't run on wheels at all. Instead, they hover above a special track, called a guideway, using strong magnets. These trains are called magnetic levitation trains, or maglevs for short.

Internet links

For links to websites where you can see maglev trains speeding along guideways and explore an animated guide to how maglev trains work, go to **www.usborne-quicklinks.com**

The fastest ever

Maglevs are still being tested, but they could soon become the fastest trains in the world. In 1999, one maglev reached a speed of 549kph (343mph) on a test track. Maglevs have been built in Japan and Germany, and they are now being developed in the U.S.A. too.

Using magnets

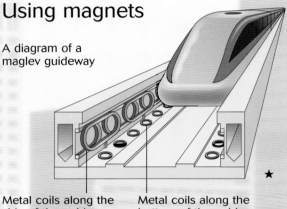

A diagram of a maglev guideway

Metal coils along the side of the guideway

Metal coils along the bottom of the guideway

Maglev guideways have metal coils along the track and on the raised sides. When electricity flows through these coils, they become very strong magnets, called electromagnets.

The electromagnets on the track create forces that push against magnets underneath the train. This lifts the train. The electromagnets on the sides of the guideway alternately pull and push magnets along the sides of the train. This propels the train forward.

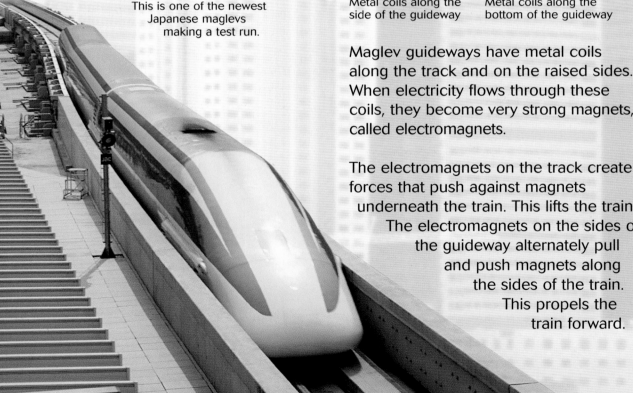

This is one of the newest Japanese maglevs making a test run.

Fact: Maglev trains are much quieter than ordinary trains because they don't touch the track. This makes the journey smoother, too.

Transrapids

German maglev trains are called Transrapids. They are designed in a different way from Japanese maglevs. The sides of a Transrapid curve around an elevated guideway. The sets of magnets that lift and propel the train forward are on the train's curved edges and underneath the guideway.

This diagram of a Transrapid shows how the train fits around the guideway.

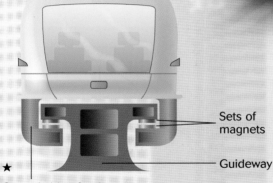

Sets of magnets

Guideway

★ Curved side of train

A computer-generated image showing what the newest Transrapid trains will look like

Into the future

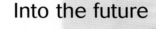

This small Japanese maglev is designed to run in cities, taking people to and from work quickly and easily.

Japanese engineers are developing maglev trains that will travel at speeds of up to 300kph (186mph) on routes between cities. Small maglevs may also be used for getting around within cities. But maglev trains may never replace ordinary trains, as the guideways could be extremely expensive to build.

Great train journeys

Railway lines have been built through some of the most spectacular scenery in the world. Here are just a few of the most impressive and exciting train journeys.

Trans-Siberian Railway

The map on the left shows the route of the Trans-Siberian Railway. Above is one of the old steam locomotives that used to run along this route.

The Trans-Siberian Railway is the world's longest railway line. It stretches from Moscow in the west of Russia to Vladivostok in the east, a distance of over 9,000km (5,600 miles). The line runs through tough terrain, including high rocky land, swamps and icy plains. The full journey takes about seven days.

The Indian Pacific

The Indian Pacific train travels all the way across Australia, from Perth on the west coast to Sydney on the opposite side of the country. This is a journey of 64 hours. Part of the route is across the Nullarbor Plain, a vast, flat desert that covers an area four times the size of Belgium. The track there runs completely straight for 478km (297 miles). It is the longest stretch of straight track in the world.

An Indian Pacific train crosses the Nullarbor Plain, a desert which gets its name from the Latin for "no trees".

Crossing the Rockies

One of the most scenic train journeys in the world is from Vancouver to Calgary in western Canada. Passengers travel on the *Rocky Mountaineer* train, which weaves through the spectacular, snow-capped Rocky Mountains.

Internet links

For links to websites where you can see video clips of train journeys through the Rockies and view an Indian Pacific carriage, go to **www.usborne-quicklinks.com**

The *Rocky Mountaineer* passenger train passing Mount Stephen in British Columbia, Canada

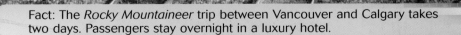

Fact: The *Rocky Mountaineer* trip between Vancouver and Calgary takes two days. Passengers stay overnight in a luxury hotel.

41

Amazing models

Model trains have existed for almost as long as real trains. The first models were clockwork toys, but later, detailed replicas of trains were made. Today, you can buy a model of just about any train you can think of.

Internet links

For links to websites where you can visit an online model train museum and take a tour of a model railroad exhibit, go to
www.usborne-quicklinks.com

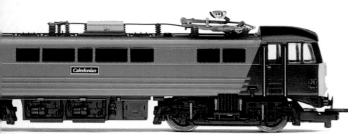
A model of a modern electric locomotive

Working to scale

Model trains and tracks are made in several sizes, or scales. Model collectors must choose just one scale, to make sure that everything is the right size in relation to everything else. One popular scale is O-scale, which makes trains 48 times smaller than the real thing. Some scales are even tinier. Z-scale models are 220 times smaller than real trains, making a Z-scale locomotive small enough to fit in the palm of your hand.

A 1940s steam locomotive model

These locomotives are made by Hornby, a British model train company. They are all OO-scale, which means they are about 23cm (9in) long.

A model of *Coronation*, a 1937 streamlined steam locomotive

A model of a modern electric locomotive

Bigger and bigger

Some model enthusiasts build enormous railway layouts. One of the biggest model railways in the world was built by an American named Bruce Williams. It has 13km (8 miles) of track and more than 300 bridges, as well as about 4,000 buildings and 500,000 trees.

This model railway has several trains that run on interlinking tracks.

Fact: Arthur Sherwood, an Australian model-maker, builds trains that are half the length of a matchstick. His trains even have tiny electric motors.

Did you know? ....

Over the years, many amazing and unusual trains have been built. Here you can find out about some of them.

✸✸ *Cycloped* was a horse-powered locomotive invented in 1829. A horse ran on a treadmill inside the locomotive to drive it forward. *Cycloped* could only reach 8kph (5mph), and went even slower when the horse got tired.

✸✸ From 1896 until 1901, a strange train on stilts ran along a beach in Brighton, on the south coast of England. The main part of the train was high above the track, so that passengers didn't get wet when the tide was in. The train was powered by electricity from an overhead cable.

✸✸ In 1880, a funicular railway was built up the side of Mount Vesuvius, a volcano in Italy. Many tourists rode on the railway and enjoyed the views from the top. But in 1943 the volcano erupted and the railway was destroyed.

Above is an Aérotrain. In test runs, these trains regularly reached speeds of more than 350kph (220mph).

✸✸ Aérotrains were invented in France in the 1960s. They hovered above the track on a cushion of air, and were powered forward by a propeller on the top of the train, driven by an aircraft engine. But only a few Aérotrains were ever made, as TGVs were developed at the same time and soon became much more widely built and used.

In the 1920s, a Scottish engineer named George Bennie created an experimental train called a Railplane. It was a monorail train powered by propellers, like a plane. Only one Railplane was ever built.

The longest passenger train ever was made up of 70 carriages, or cars. It was pulled by an electric locomotive and ran in Belgium in 1991.

One of the most streamlined trains is the new Japanese bullet train. The front of the train is so pointed that there is hardly any room for the driver.

In snowy places, such as Alaska, special locomotives are used to clear railway lines. As the locomotive moves along, huge blades on the front spin around, whipping the snow off the track.

Some electric city trains don't have drivers. Instead they are operated by computers, which make sure that the trains stay a safe distance apart.

The fastest vehicle ever to run on rails was rocket-powered and driverless. In 1982, it reached a speed of 9,851kph (6,121mph), which is eight times the speed of sound.

The pointed nose of this new bullet train is 15m (50ft) long. Its narrow shape helps it to cut through the air easily.

45

Internet links.....................................

Throughout this book we have recommended websites where you can find out more about trains. To visit the sites, go to the **Usborne Quicklinks Website** where you will find links to all the sites.

1. Go to **www.usborne-quicklinks.com**
2. Type the keywords for this book: **discovery trains**
3. Type the page number of the link you want to visit.
4. Click on the link to go to the recommended site.

Here are some of the things you can do on the websites recommended in this book:
- Watch video clips of stream trains.
- Build The Rocket online and find out how it worked.
- Take a virtual tour of an American diesel locomotive.
- Watch a slide show about bullet trains.

Site availability

The links in Usborne Quicklinks are regularly reviewed and updated, but occasionally you may get a message that a site is unavailable. This might be temporary, so try again later, or even the next day. Websites do occasionally close down and when this happens, we will replace them with new links in Usborne Quicklinks. Sometimes we add extra links too, if we think they are useful. So when you visit Usborne Quicklinks, the links may be slightly different from those described in your book.

Downloadable pictures

Pictures marked with a ★ in this book can be downloaded from the Usborne Quicklinks Website. These pictures are for personal use only and must not be used for commercial purposes.

> **COMPUTER NOT ESSENTIAL**
> If you don't have access to the internet, don't worry. This book is a fun and informative introduction to trains.

Safety on the internet

Ask your parent's or guardian's permission before you connect to the internet and make sure you follow these simple rules:

- Never give out information about yourself, such as your real name, address, phone number or the name of your school.
- If a site asks you to log in or register by typing your name or email address, ask permission from an adult first.

What you need

To visit the websites you need a computer with an internet connection and a web browser (the software that lets you look at information from the internet). Some sites need extra programs (plug-ins) to play sound or show videos or animations.

If you go to a site and do not have the necessary plug-in, a message will come up on the screen. There is usually a link to click on to download the plug-in. For more information about plug-ins, go to Usborne Quicklinks and click on "Net Help".

Notes for parents and guardians

The websites described in this book are regularly reviewed, but the content of a website may change at any time and Usborne Publishing is not responsible for the content on any website other than its own.

We recommend that children are supervised while on the internet, that they do not use Internet chat rooms, and that you use Internet filtering software to block unsuitable material. Please ensure that your children read and follow the safety guidelines printed above. For more information, see the Net Help area on the Usborne Quicklinks Website.

Index ....

Acknowledgements......................................

Every effort has been made to trace the copyright holders of the material in this book. If any rights have been omitted, the publishers offer to rectify this in any subsequent editions following notification. The publishers are grateful to the following organizations and individuals for their permission to reproduce material (t=top, m=middle, b=bottom, l=left, r=right):

Cover © W.A. Sharman; Milepost 92½/CORBIS, © John Russell; **p1** © Robert Holmes/CORBIS; **p2–3** © Ric Ergenbright/CORBIS; **p4–5t** © Mark Brayford/Milepost 92½; **p4b** © TRH/D Burrows; **p5b** © Powerstock Zefa; **p6–7m** © TRH/A Barnes; **p6t** © Bettmann/CORBIS; **p6bl** © National Railway Museum/Science & Society; **p8b** © Alan Pike/Milepost 92½; **p9t** © Milepost 92½; **p10–11 background** © Joseph Sohm: Visions of America/CORBIS; **p10b** © Ron Ruhoff/Powerstock Zefa; **p11** © Wolfgang Kaehler/CORBIS; **p12–13b** © National Railway Museum/Science & Society; **p13tr** © Bettmann/CORBIS; **p14bl** © Venice Simplon-Orient-Express Ltd; **p15** © National Railway Museum/ Science & Society; **p16tr** © G. A. Cryer; **p16b** © Museum of the City of New York/CORBIS; **p17br** © Neil Wheelwright/Milepost 92½; **p18b, tunnel** © Powerstock Zefa; **p18b, train** © Colin Garratt, Milepost 92½/CORBIS; **p19t** © Arnold Jon/ The Photographers Library; **p19br** © Robert Holmes/ CORBIS; **p20b** © Tony Morrison/South American Pictures; **p21tr** © Sandro Vannini/CORBIS; **p21br** © Michel Azema/Funimag; **p22m** © A. J. Hurst; **p23m** © National Railway Museum/Science & Society; **p24–25b** © Thomas Konz; **p24tr** © Werner Krutein/Photovault; **p25tr** © National Railway Museum/Science & Society; **p26–27b** © Union Pacific Historical Collection; **p26t** © Colin Garratt, Milepost 92½/CORBIS; **p27mr** © Colin Garratt, Milepost 92½/CORBIS; **p28–29b** © Union Pacific Historical Collection; **p29mr** © Hulton-Deutsch Collection/ CORBIS; **p30ml** © Stefano Paolini/ Photorail; **p30–31m** © Michael S. Yamashita/CORBIS; **p31b** © Yann Nottara; **p32–33b** © Colin Garratt/Milepost 92½; **p33tr** © TRH/A Barnes; **p34tr** © Jim Byrne/ QAPHOTOS; **p34br** © Diana Craigie/QAPHOTOS; **p35b** © Bill Ross/CORBIS; **p36–37t** © Clem Tillier/TGVWeb; **p37b** © Bill Ross/ CORBIS; **p38–39 background** © Neil Rabinowitz/CORBIS; **p38bl** © Dr. A. J. Finch/Milepost 92½; **p39tr** © Michael S. Yamashita/CORBIS; **p39br** © Transrapid International; **p40tr** © Railfotos/Millbrook House Limited; **p40b** © Commonwealth of Australia, reproduced by permission of the National Archives of Australia; **p41** © Scott Rowed/Rocky Mountaineer Railtours; **p42 & 43 all** © Hornby Hobbies Ltd, reproduced by kind permission, all rights reserved; **p44tr** © John Dominis/Powerstock Zefa; **p44–45br** © Dr. A. J. Finch/Milepost 92½.

Series editor: Gillian Doherty; Managing editor: Jane Chisholm; Managing designer: Mary Cartwright Photographic manipulation: John Russell, Roger Bolton and Andrea Slane; Cover design: Zoe Wray and Helen Edmonds